THE NIGHT AS PATH

DREAMS, ILLUSION, AND RECOGNITION IN
TIBETAN BUDDHISM

QUYEN NGO

Copyright © 2026 by Quyen Ngo

All rights reserved.

No part of this book may be reproduced in any form or by any electronic or mechanical means, including information storage and retrieval systems, without written permission from the author, except for brief quotations in reviews.

Published by Pana Mind Press

CONTENTS

Preface   v

Author's Note   1
Introduction: Why Tibetan Buddhism Trains the Dreaming Mind   3
Chapter 1: Illusion and Awakening in Tibetan Buddhism   8
Chapter 2: The Subtle Mind and the Continuity of Awareness   14
Chapter 3: Dreams as a Yogic Field   20
Chapter 4: Ethical Ground and Motivation   25
Chapter 5: Attention and Stability   30
Chapter 6: The First Moment of Recognition   36
Chapter 7: Remaining Within the Dream   41
Chapter 8: Transformation Without Manipulation   46
Chapter 9: Limits, Risks, and Misunderstandings   51
Chapter 10: Integration: When the Night Informs the Day   56
Conclusion: The Night as Path   61
A Note to the Reader   65

Notes   67

PREFACE

This book is not a manual.

It does not offer techniques for mastering dreams, inducing lucidity, or bending experience to intention. It does not promise transformation through control. Those expectations, common in contemporary accounts of dream practice, miss what Tibetan dream yoga is most carefully concerned with.

Dreams are treated here as a place where experience shows its seams.

In the night, belief forms quickly. Identity assembles with little resistance. Fear persuades without argument. Desire directs without explanation. Recognition appears briefly, often without warning, and just as easily disappears. What unfolds in dreams is not separate from waking life. It is simply more condensed, more exposed.

This book moves slowly through that exposure.

Rather than approaching dream yoga as a way of altering what appears, the chapters that follow attend to how recognition arises, fades, and is met again through restraint. Dreams are not treated

Preface

as puzzles to solve or environments to manipulate. They are treated as a field in which the habits of experience can be observed as they form.

The emphasis throughout is on orientation rather than instruction.

Readers looking for methods may find this approach spare. Readers willing to remain with uncertainty may find it clarifying. The work asks for attention rather than effort, and for patience rather than intervention.

Dream yoga, as understood here, is not an escape from life. It is a way of learning how life persuades, both in the night and in the daylight that follows.

AUTHOR'S NOTE

This book emerged from sustained engagement with contemplative practice and scholarship, as well as a long-standing interest in how experience comes to feel convincing.

It deliberately avoids organizing dream yoga around biography, lineage, or exemplary figures. Such figures matter deeply within Tibetan traditions, but this book is concerned with something quieter: the movement of recognition, the return of control, and the fragile interval in which belief loosens.

No specialized knowledge is assumed. At the same time, the material is not simplified in order to reassure. The practice described here is subtle and approached without haste.

Tibetan sources are drawn on where clarity requires them, but the aim is not comprehensive coverage. The aim is coherence. What matters is not how much is included, but how carefully it is held.

If the book succeeds, it will do so without announcement. Not by persuading, but by making persuasion visible. Not by resolving uncertainty, but by staying with it long enough for its shape to appear.

QUYEN NGO

The night becomes a path only when it is not grasped. This book is offered in that spirit.

INTRODUCTION: WHY TIBETAN BUDDHISM TRAINS THE DREAMING MIND

When the world goes dark and the body lies down, most of what we call practice quietly stops.

The senses withdraw. Speech ends. Intention loosens.

Sleep arrives.

For many Buddhist traditions, this is where training pauses. Night is for rest. The mind is allowed to wander, dream, and dissolve, to be gathered again the next morning. Dreams, in this view, are side effects of a sleeping body. Interesting, sometimes revealing, but ultimately unreliable. Something to be restrained or ignored rather than deliberately cultivated.

Tibetan Buddhism takes a different position.

It begins from a simple observation: the mind does not stop when we fall asleep. It continues to form worlds, identities, fears, and desires with remarkable speed and coherence. The same habits that shape waking perception reappear at night, often more vividly, because the usual constraints of the external world have fallen away.

Rather than treating this as a problem, Tibetan Buddhist traditions treat it as an opportunity.

Dream yoga arises from the recognition that if illusion governs waking life, it governs the night as well. And if illusion can be recognized in one state, it can be recognized in another. The dream is not a distraction from the path. It is a field in which the path can be trained.

This book explores that field.

A Different Use of Dreams

In Tibetan Buddhism, dreams are not primarily interpreted. They are used.

Not as omens, and not as symbolic puzzles to be decoded, but as living experiences in which insight can be cultivated directly.

Dream yoga rests on a particular understanding of mind and reality. According to this view, appearances are neither denied nor taken at face value. What we experience is real in the sense that it is felt, inhabited, and consequential. But it is not real in the sense of being fixed, independent, or self-existing.

Dreams make this visible with unusual clarity.

In a dream, a world appears fully formed. A self appears within it. Fear, joy, longing, and confusion arise as convincingly as they do during the day. Yet when the dream ends, the entire structure dissolves, leaving no residue. Nothing has traveled anywhere. Nothing has been destroyed. The mind has simply changed state.

For Tibetan practitioners, this is not merely a metaphor. It is training material.

Dream yoga takes the instability of the dream world and turns it into a laboratory for insight. The looseness of appearances, the speed with which identities form and dissolve, and the reduced grip of the physical senses make dreams a uniquely fertile space for recognizing how experience is constructed.

The aim is not control.

It is recognition.

Scope and Intention of This Book

This book is a tradition-specific exploration of Tibetan Buddhist dream yoga. It is grounded explicitly in Vajrayāna assumptions about mind, illusion, and awakening. It treats dream yoga as a deliberate contemplative discipline, not as a curiosity, a psychological technique, or a symbolic art.

Because of this, it is important to be clear about what the book is —and what it is not.

This is not a general Buddhist treatment of dreams.

It is not a continuation or completion of early Buddhist teachings.

It is not a claim that dream yoga represents a higher or final path.

And it is not a how-to manual stripped of ethical, philosophical, or lineage context.

Dream yoga only makes sense within a particular framework: one that assumes continuity of awareness across waking, dreaming, and sleep; one that treats illusion as something to be trained with, not merely understood conceptually; and one that places ethical motivation and humility at the center of practice.

Without this framework, dream yoga is easily distorted into entertainment, ego inflation, or spiritual ambition. This book is written to prevent that misunderstanding.

. . .

Illusion as Training, Not Escape

A common misunderstanding of dream yoga is that it encourages withdrawal from ordinary life or fascination with altered states. In fact, its logic points in the opposite direction.

The purpose of recognizing illusion is not to dismiss the world, but to relate to it more clearly. Illusion, in this context, does not mean that nothing matters. It means that what appears is not as solid as it seems, and that suffering arises when appearances are taken as fixed and self-defining.

Dreams offer a concentrated version of this process. Fear arises quickly. Identity shifts easily. Entire situations form and collapse without effort. When awareness is present within this movement, the mind learns—not through theory, but through experience—how to remain steady amid change.

This learning does not remain confined to the night.

One of the defining features of Tibetan dream yoga is that it is never practiced in isolation. It is continuous with daytime awareness, ethical conduct, and contemplative stability. The aim is not to become skilled at dreaming, but to weaken the reflex of taking appearances as absolute, wherever they arise.

How This Book Is Structured

The chapters that follow move from view to practice, and from practice to integration.

The first part establishes the philosophical and experiential basis for dream yoga: why illusion matters, how the subtle mind is understood, and why dreams provide a uniquely powerful field for training insight.

The middle sections explore how lucidity is cultivated, what it reveals, and how dream experience is transformed without reinforcing control or ego. These chapters emphasize lived phenomenology over instruction—what practitioners notice, struggle with, and gradually learn to let go of.

The final part addresses integration and caution. Dream yoga is not risk-free, and it is not appropriate for every temperament or motivation. Misunderstandings are common, and humility is essential. The goal is not extraordinary experience, but a quieter, more flexible relationship to experience itself.

Orientation

Dream yoga does not ask the practitioner to reject the world.

It asks them to see how the world appears.

By training awareness in the most unstable of states, Tibetan Buddhism makes a restrained but radical claim: awakening is not confined to posture, place, or time of day. If illusion can be recognized in the dream, it can be recognized anywhere. And if it can be recognized anywhere, it no longer needs to be feared.

The chapters that follow explore how this recognition is cultivated—carefully, deliberately, and with respect for both the power and the limits of the practice.

CHAPTER 1: ILLUSION AND AWAKENING IN TIBETAN BUDDHISM

The word *illusion* carries a quiet danger.

It suggests trickery, dismissal, or escape.

Something unreal that can be waved away once it is recognized.

Tibetan Buddhism does not use the term so lightly.

When Tibetan texts describe the world as dreamlike or illusory, they are not claiming that experience is meaningless or that nothing truly appears. They are pointing to something subtler and more difficult to see: that appearances arise dependently, lack fixed essence, and are continuously shaped by the habits of mind that encounter them.

Illusion, in this sense, is not an error to be corrected.

It is a condition to be understood.

This distinction matters because dream yoga rests entirely upon it. Without a clear view of illusion, the practice becomes either trivial or dangerous. Trivial, if dreams are treated as mere entertainment. Dangerous, if illusion is mistaken for nihilism or detachment.

The Tibetan approach avoids both.

Illusion Without Denial

In the Tibetan Buddhist view, appearances are neither rejected nor absolutized. They are taken seriously, precisely because they are experienced. Pain hurts. Fear constricts. Desire pulls. Compassion opens. None of this is denied. What is questioned is not the presence of experience, but the assumptions that quietly attach to it.

We assume that what appears is solid.

We assume that it stands on its own.

We assume that the self who experiences it is equally solid and equally independent.

These assumptions operate so quickly that they feel invisible. They do not announce themselves as beliefs. They present themselves as common sense.

Dreams interrupt this certainty.

In a dream, an entire world appears without external support. Landscapes unfold. Characters speak. A body moves, suffers, desires, and reacts. The experience is complete, immersive, and convincing. Yet the moment of waking reveals how provisional the whole structure was. Nothing needed to be dismantled. It simply ceased.

Tibetan Buddhism does not treat this as a curiosity. It treats it as an instruction.

The dream shows, in condensed form, what is always happening. Appearances arise. Meaning is assigned. Identity forms in response. And all of it depends on conditions that are rarely examined.

Illusion, then, does not mean that nothing appears.

It means that what appears does not appear as we think it does.

Emptiness as Lived Insight

The Tibetan understanding of illusion is inseparable from emptiness. But emptiness here is not a metaphysical claim. It is not a statement about what ultimately exists. It is a way of describing how experience functions when examined closely.

To say that phenomena are empty is to say that they lack an independent essence. They arise in dependence on causes, conditions, and perception. They are real as experiences, but unstable as entities.

This insight is often grasped intellectually long before it is embodied. One can understand emptiness conceptually and still react to the world as if nothing had changed. Fear still grips. Desire still convinces. Identity still hardens.

Dream yoga exists because Tibetan Buddhism does not assume that understanding alone is sufficient.

If illusion is woven into perception itself, then it must be encountered where perception is most fluid. Dreams offer that encounter. In dreams, the mind reveals its habits without the usual protections of the waking world. Reactions unfold faster. Attachments are exaggerated. Identity is more malleable.

This is not a weakness of dreams. It is their strength.

Why Illusion Must Be Trained

A recurring theme in Tibetan Buddhist practice is that insight must be stabilized. Recognition, on its own, is fragile. It appears briefly, then vanishes under pressure. The mind returns to familiar patterns, not because insight was false, but because habit is strong.

Dream yoga addresses this directly.

In waking life, appearances resist transformation. Physical laws impose limits. Social roles reinforce identity. Consequences unfold slowly. In dreams, these constraints loosen. Forms change easily. Fear escalates quickly. Identity shifts without warning.

This makes the dream state uniquely suited for training recognition.

When a practitioner becomes lucid in a dream, something subtle occurs. The dream does not disappear. The world continues. Characters speak. Events unfold. What changes is the relationship to what appears. The dream is experienced as an appearance rather than as an absolute reality.

This recognition is not abstract. It is immediate and embodied. The practitioner sees, directly, how conviction gives way when solidity is questioned.

Over time, this recognition leaves an imprint. The mind learns that certainty is optional. That appearances can be engaged without being believed in the way they once were. That fear loses some of its authority when its constructed nature is seen.

This learning does not remain confined to dreams.

The Continuity of Confusion and Insight

Tibetan Buddhism emphasizes continuity across states. Waking, dreaming, and sleep are not treated as separate domains governed by different laws. They are expressions of the same mind, operating under different conditions.

Confusion continues across these states. So does insight.

This is why dream yoga is not introduced as an isolated technique. It is integrated into a larger path of ethical discipline, meditative stability, and philosophical clarity. Without this foundation, dream practice becomes distorted. Lucidity turns into control. Insight turns into fascination.

The training is not aimed at producing extraordinary experiences. It is aimed at weakening reflexive belief.

In this sense, illusion is not something to escape from. It is something to work with. The dream becomes a place where the mind's habits are revealed, challenged, and gradually softened.

Awakening Without Escape

A persistent misunderstanding about illusion is that recognizing it leads away from ordinary life. That once appearances are seen as dreamlike, engagement loses its meaning. Tibetan Buddhism rejects this conclusion.

Recognition does not remove appearance.

It removes fixation.

When illusion is understood, the world does not become distant or irrelevant. It becomes workable. Responses loosen. Compassion becomes less obstructed by fear. Responsibility deepens rather than dissolves.

Dream yoga trains this capacity under conditions where the mind is least defended. It is a demanding practice precisely because it does not allow the practitioner to hide behind concepts. The dream responds immediately. Fear appears when fear is present. Desire exposes itself without disguise.

There is nowhere to stand outside the experience. Only awareness within it.

. . .

Setting the Ground for Practice

Before any discussion of technique, this view must be clear. Dream yoga does not function as a shortcut to awakening. It does not bypass ethical discipline, emotional maturity, or philosophical grounding. It intensifies them.

Illusion, when misunderstood, leads to carelessness.

Illusion, when understood properly, leads to responsibility.

The chapters that follow build from this view. They do not rush toward lucidity. They begin by establishing the conditions under which lucidity becomes meaningful. The training of attention, motivation, and restraint precedes any attempt to work consciously with dreams.

Without this order, the practice collapses into confusion.

With it, the dream becomes what Tibetan Buddhism has long claimed it to be: not an escape from the path, but one of its most revealing terrains.

CHAPTER 2: THE SUBTLE MIND AND THE CONTINUITY OF AWARENESS

When Tibetan Buddhism speaks about dream yoga, it does not begin with dreams.

It begins with the mind that dreams.

This is an important distinction. Dreams are not treated as isolated events that occur during sleep, nor as symbolic by-products of bodily rest. They are understood as expressions of a continuity of awareness that persists across waking, dreaming, and deep sleep. Without this assumption, dream yoga would make little sense. With it, the practice becomes coherent.

The Tibetan Buddhist account of the mind is layered rather than singular. Ordinary waking consciousness is only one mode among several. Beneath it lie subtler levels of awareness, less dependent on sensory input and less constrained by the structures that govern daytime experience. These subtler modes do not appear suddenly at death or in meditation. They are already present. Sleep reveals them.

Gross and Subtle Consciousness

In everyday life, attention is largely absorbed by the senses. Perception is anchored to sight, sound, touch, and movement. The world appears stable because the sensory field is stable, and identity feels continuous because the body provides constant reference points.

As the body falls asleep, this anchoring weakens.

Sensory input fades. Volitional control loosens. Conceptual thought slows, though it does not disappear. What remains is a mode of awareness that is more fluid, less bounded, and more responsive to internal conditions than external ones. Tibetan traditions describe this transition as a movement from gross to subtle consciousness.[1]

This does not mean that the subtle mind is mysterious or rare. It is simply less obvious during waking life, overshadowed by sensory engagement and habitual conceptual activity. Dreaming offers one of the clearest daily encounters with this subtler mode.

From the Tibetan perspective, this matters because insight is not confined to one level of the mind. If awakening involves recognizing the nature of experience, then it must involve the modes of mind in which experience continues when the senses withdraw.

Dream yoga rests on this premise.

Continuity Across States

A key feature of Tibetan Buddhist thought is the insistence on continuity. Waking, dreaming, and sleep are not treated as separate compartments, each governed by different rules. They are expressions of the same stream of awareness, shaped by different conditions.

Confusion carries across these states. So does clarity.

Habits of grasping do not disappear at night. They reorganize themselves. Fear finds new forms. Desire invents new scenarios. Identity reconstitutes itself with remarkable speed. The fact that these patterns appear so vividly in dreams is not accidental. It reveals how deeply they are ingrained.

At the same time, moments of recognition can also arise in dreams. Awareness can register the constructed nature of what appears. This recognition does not require waking cognition. It arises from the same capacity that operates during the day, now freed from many external constraints.

This continuity is central to Vajrayāna practice more broadly. Tibetan traditions often emphasize the transitions between states, seeing them as moments when habitual perception is destabilized, and insight becomes possible. Sleep and dreaming are among the most accessible of these transitions, encountered daily rather than reserved for exceptional circumstances.[2]

Dreams and the Subtle Body

Tibetan explanations of dreaming are closely linked to teachings on the subtle body. While details vary across lineages, the general framework is consistent: consciousness is understood to move through channels, energies, and centers that shape experience at different levels. Dreaming corresponds to shifts within this subtle system, particularly as sensory engagement withdraws and internal processes come to the foreground.[3]

It is important to approach these teachings carefully. They are not speculative physiology, nor are they meant to function as literal anatomy. They are experiential maps, developed to describe patterns observed through long contemplative practice.

For the purposes of dream yoga, the key point is not the mechanics themselves, but the implication they carry. If consciousness can function independently of gross sensory input, then awareness does not belong exclusively to waking life. It can operate under far more subtle conditions.

Dream yoga trains recognition within those conditions.

Sleep, Dream, and Death

Tibetan Buddhist texts frequently draw parallels between sleep, dreaming, and the process of dying. This comparison is not meant to be dramatic or morbid. It reflects a shared structure. In each case, sensory engagement dissolves, ordinary identity loosens, and subtler modes of awareness come forward.

Dreaming occupies an intermediate position within this sequence. It is less destabilizing than death and more accessible than deep meditative absorption. Precisely because of this, it offers a practical training ground.

The point, however, is not preparation in a literal or guaranteed sense. Dream yoga does not promise control over death or certainty in intermediate states. Tibetan sources repeatedly caution against such expectations.[4] What dream practice can offer is familiarity. A mind that has learned to recognize appearance as appearance is less likely to be overwhelmed when familiar reference points dissolve.

This is one reason dream yoga emphasizes continuity rather than mastery. The aim is not to dominate experience, but to remain oriented within it.

The Subtle Mind as Training Ground

Dreams reveal the subtle mind in motion. They show how quickly perception organizes itself into meaning, how readily identity forms, and how reflexively the mind reacts to what it takes to be real.

In waking life, these processes are slow enough to seem solid. In dreams, they accelerate. Fear escalates instantly. Attachment convinces without hesitation. Confusion compounds itself with little resistance.

For dream yoga, this acceleration is not a flaw. It is a feature.

When awareness is present within the dream, the practitioner encounters the mechanics of illusion directly. The speed of construction becomes visible. The absence of external constraint exposes the mind's creative and reactive tendencies with unusual clarity.

This is why dream yoga is not introduced as an advanced add-on. It depends on prior stability, ethical grounding, and clarity of view. Without these, the subtle mind amplifies confusion rather than insight.

With them, the dream becomes a precise and demanding field of training.

Preparing for Practice

The continuity of awareness described in this chapter sets the stage for what follows. Dream yoga does not begin by trying to induce lucidity. It begins by establishing conditions in which recognition can arise without strain.

These conditions include ethical discipline, attentional stability, and motivation that is not driven by fascination or ambition. Without them, the subtle mind simply reflects existing tendencies more vividly.

The next chapter turns to this foundation. Before lucidity is cultivated, the ground must be prepared. The training of the dreaming mind begins long before sleep.

CHAPTER 3: DREAMS AS A YOGIC FIELD

Dream yoga does not begin with technique.

It begins with a decision about where training will take place.

In Tibetan Buddhism, dreams are treated as a field of practice, not because they are extraordinary, but because they are ordinary. They arise nightly, without special conditions, and they reveal the mind at work when its usual supports have fallen away. This makes them unusually honest. The dream does not conceal habit. It exposes it.

What matters is not that dreams are strange, but that they are immediate. Fear, attachment, and identity appear without delay. The mind does not have time to edit itself. For practice, this immediacy is invaluable.

A yogic field is not a location. It is a context in which training can occur. Dreams become such a context when they are approached not as messages to be interpreted, but as experiences to be inhabited with awareness.

Why Dreams Are Used

From the Tibetan perspective, the dream state offers three conditions that are difficult to reproduce during waking life.

First, appearances are fluid. Forms change easily. Environments shift without resistance. Identity is unstable. This fluidity allows for real-time construction observation, rather than inferring it afterward.

Second, emotional responses are intensified. Fear escalates quickly. Desire persuades without hesitation. Aversion solidifies before reflection can intervene. These reactions are not distortions of waking life. They are compressions of it. The same tendencies are present during the day, but they unfold more slowly and are easier to rationalize.

Third, the sense of consequence is altered. Actions in dreams feel meaningful while they occur, yet their outcomes dissolve upon waking. This creates a space in which the grip of outcome is weakened, even as experience remains vivid.

Taken together, these conditions make dreams an ideal environment for working with recognition. They allow the practitioner to encounter illusion not as an abstract principle, but as lived experience.

Tibetan texts repeatedly emphasize that this is not incidental. Dreams are used because they accelerate the display of the mind.[1]

The Difference Between Observation and Practice

It is important to distinguish between noticing dreams and practicing within them. Many traditions acknowledge that dreams reflect mental states. Tibetan Buddhism goes further. It treats the dream itself as a site of intentional training.

This shift is subtle but decisive.

To observe a dream is to reflect on it after the fact. To practice within a dream is to engage awareness as the experience unfolds. The difference is not analytical. It is temporal. Practice occurs in the moment of appearance, not in retrospect.

This is why dream yoga is inseparable from the cultivation of attentional stability during the day. Without some capacity to remain present amid changing experience, the dream simply carries the practitioner along. Awareness arrives too late, if it arrives at all.

The goal is not constant lucidity. Tibetan sources are clear on this point. Even experienced practitioners may pass through long periods without recognizable dream awareness. What matters is the gradual weakening of automatic belief.[2]

Dreams become a yogic field not when they are controlled, but when they are met with recognition, however briefly.

Working With Illusion Directly

In Chapter 1, illusion was described as a condition to be understood rather than an error to be corrected. Dreams make this understanding operational.

Within a dream, the practitioner encounters appearances that compel belief. The body reacts. Emotion intensifies. Narrative coherence asserts itself. All of this happens before reflective thought can intervene. When recognition arises within this momentum, it does not dismantle the dream. It changes the relationship to it.

Fear may still be present, but it no longer defines the field. Desire may still appear, but its authority weakens. The dream continues, yet the compulsion to take it as absolute loosens.

This is the core training of dream yoga. It does not aim to remove illusion. It aims to see through it while it functions.

Tibetan commentarial traditions often stress that this recognition must be gentle. Aggressive attempts to impose awareness tend to fragment the dream or collapse it entirely. The practice is not to interrupt experience, but to remain present within it.[3]

Rehearsal Without Simulation

Dream yoga is sometimes described as rehearsal for waking life. This description is only partially accurate.

The dream is not a simulation of waking experience. It is a more concentrated expression of the same dynamics. What appears in dreams is not symbolic in the ordinary sense. It is functional. The same patterns of grasping, aversion, and confusion operate, but without the buffering effect of physical constraint.

Because of this, the dream offers a unique opportunity to work with difficult states. Fear, in particular, becomes accessible in a way that is often unavailable during the day. In waking life, fear is frequently avoided, suppressed, or managed indirectly. In dreams, it must be faced.

Tibetan sources consistently describe the use of fear in dream practice, not as an ordeal, but as a means of softening fixation. When fear is recognized as an appearance, its solidity diminishes. This recognition carries forward into waking life, where fear tends to operate more covertly.[4]

The dream, then, is not rehearsed in order to perform better later. It is engaged in order to understand how experience persuades.

Limits and Constraints

Treating dreams as a yogic field does not mean that anything goes. Tibetan traditions are explicit about the limits of dream practice.

Dream yoga is not introduced early in training. It presupposes ethical discipline, emotional stability, and a motivation oriented toward insight rather than power. Without these conditions, the dream amplifies existing tendencies rather than transforming them.

This is one reason Tibetan texts repeatedly caution against fascination with lucidity. The ability to alter dream content is not evidence of progress. It can just as easily reinforce subtle forms of control and identity.

The yogic value of the dream lies not in its manipulability, but in its transparency. When the dream is treated as a field of practice, the emphasis remains on recognition, not authorship.

From Field to Path

By treating dreams as a yogic field, Tibetan Buddhism makes a quiet but consequential claim: practice does not require special circumstances. It requires the willingness to meet experience where it already unfolds.

Dreams offer this meeting nightly. They do not wait for retreat conditions or ideal mental states. They arise regardless of intention. When approached skillfully, they become a continuation of the path rather than an interruption.

The chapters that follow turn toward preparation. Before lucidity is addressed directly, the conditions that support recognition must be clarified. Dream yoga does not begin at night. It begins with how attention is trained during the day.

CHAPTER 4: ETHICAL GROUND AND MOTIVATION

Dream yoga does not begin at night.

It begins with how a person lives during the day.

This is not a preliminary caution added for completeness. It is a structural claim. Tibetan traditions are consistent on this point: without ethical ground and clear motivation, dream practice does not merely fail to mature. It turns unstable.

The reason is simple. Dreams amplify what is already present. They do not correct it.

As shown in earlier chapters, the dream state accelerates the display of habit. Emotional patterns appear quickly. Identity forms without resistance. The subtle mind reflects the tendencies that shape waking life, stripped of many external constraints. Ethics, in this context, are not rules imposed from outside. They are the conditions that determine what appears when control is weakest.

Ethics as Stabilization

In Tibetan Buddhism, ethical discipline is not treated as moral perfection. It is treated as stabilization. A mind that habitually harms, deceives, or indulges fixation cannot remain steady when appearances intensify. Dreams expose this instability without negotiation.

This is why classical Tibetan presentations of dream yoga place ethical conduct early, often before any discussion of lucidity.[1] The issue is not purity. It is coherence.

When actions during the day are aligned with restraint and care, the dream state reflects that alignment. When they are not, the dream magnifies contradiction. The practitioner is confronted, not with symbolic punishment, but with the consequences of unresolved tendencies.

This confrontation is not punitive. It is instructive.

Motivation and Its Consequences

Motivation determines the direction of practice. Tibetan sources are explicit that dream yoga pursued for fascination, entertainment, or personal power becomes counterproductive. The dream responds to such motivations by reinforcing subtle forms of control and identity.

This risk is not hypothetical. The capacity to influence dream content can arise relatively early, especially for practitioners with strong imaginative faculties. Without clear orientation, this capacity is easily mistaken for progress.[2]

Tibetan traditions counter this tendency by repeatedly returning to motivation grounded in liberation rather than acquisition. The aim is not to dominate experience, but to understand its nature. When motivation shifts toward display or mastery, the dream ceases to function as a field of recognition and becomes a stage for self-confirmation.

This distinction explains why humility is emphasized so strongly in dream yoga lineages. Humility here does not mean self-effacement. It means recognizing the limits of control and the ease with which insight can be replaced by performance.

Restraint and the Night Mind

Restraint plays a specific role in dream practice. During waking life, restraint limits the outward expression of impulse. At night, it limits the reaction's momentum.

A mind trained in restraint does not react as violently when fear appears. Desire still arises, but it does not immediately dictate response. This creates the minimal space required for recognition to occur.

Tibetan commentarial sources often describe restraint as a form of kindness toward the mind.[3] Rather than forcing awareness into difficult states, restraint reduces the frequency with which such states dominate. The dream then becomes workable rather than overwhelming.

This is one reason dream yoga is rarely taught in isolation. It is embedded within a broader discipline that shapes how the practitioner relates to experience across states.

Emotional Maturity and Dream Practice

Ethical ground also includes emotional maturity. Dreams reveal emotional material that is often managed or avoided during the day. Without some capacity to tolerate discomfort, dream practice becomes destabilizing.

Fear is particularly relevant. As noted earlier, fear appears vividly in dreams. Tibetan texts do not suggest eliminating fear before practice. They emphasize learning how to remain present with it.

This capacity is developed gradually through ethical consistency and contemplative stability, not through dream work alone.[4]

When emotional reactivity dominates waking life, dreams intensify it. When emotional responsiveness has been cultivated, dreams become a place where fear can be met without collapse.

This distinction explains why Tibetan sources repeatedly caution against premature engagement with dream practice. The issue is not technical readiness. It is readiness in temperament.

Responsibility and Continuity

A defining feature of Tibetan dream yoga is the assumption of responsibility across states. Actions during the day shape the dream. Attitudes in the dream shape waking perception. Nothing is isolated.

This continuity reinforces the ethical dimension of practice. There is no private space where consequences do not reach. The dream reflects the mind as it is trained, not as it is intended.

For this reason, Tibetan teachers often describe dream practice as unforgiving but fair. It does not flatter. It does not conceal. It reveals alignment or lack of it with unusual clarity.

This clarity is not meant to judge. It is meant to orient.

Ethics Without Moralism

It is important to note what ethical ground is not. It is not adherence to a rigid code. It is not moral superiority. It is not self-surveillance.

Ethics, in this context, function as preparation. They reduce friction in the mind. They simplify the internal environment so that recognition can arise without force.

This understanding distinguishes Tibetan dream yoga from approaches that seek extraordinary experience without attending to the conditions that support it. Tibetan traditions are explicit that insight divorced from conduct becomes unstable.[5]

Dream yoga intensifies this principle. Because the dream strips away external structure, whatever remains must be workable on its own.

Preparing the Way Forward

The ethical and motivational grounds described here do not replace practice. It makes practice possible. Without it, the dream remains a mirror of confusion. With it, the dream becomes transparent.

The next chapter turns toward attentional training. Before lucidity is addressed, attention must learn how to remain steady without rigidity. Dream practice does not demand constant awareness. It requires the capacity to return.

That capacity is cultivated first in waking life.

CHAPTER 5: ATTENTION AND STABILITY

Dream yoga does not ask for constant awareness.

It asks for recoverable awareness.

This distinction is easy to miss. Many approaches to contemplative training assume that progress is measured by continuity: how long attention can be held, how rarely it slips, how steadily awareness remains present. Tibetan dream yoga is oriented differently. What matters is not unbroken attention, but the ability to return without agitation.

This capacity is cultivated first in waking life.

As established in earlier chapters, dreams intensify habit, emotion, and identity. Ethical ground and motivation shape what appears. Attention determines whether recognition can occur at all. Without some degree of stability, the dream simply carries the practitioner along. Awareness may flicker briefly, but it cannot remain.

What Stability Means Here

Stability, in this context, does not mean rigidity. It does not require narrowing attention or suppressing mental movement. Tibetan sources consistently warn against forcing the mind into stillness, especially for practices involving subtle states.[1]

Instead, stability refers to a mind that does not immediately fragment when experience changes. A stable mind can remain oriented even as images shift, emotions intensify, or narrative coherence dissolves. It does not cling to a single object. It remains available.

This kind of stability is not produced by control. It is produced by familiarity.

Through repeated contact with distraction, return becomes easier. Attention learns that it can release fixation without collapsing. Over time, this capacity carries into sleep.

Attention Across States

Tibetan Buddhism treats attention as continuous across waking and dreaming, even though its expression changes. During the day, attention is supported by posture, intention, and sensory engagement. At night, these supports fall away. What remains is whatever capacity has been internalized.

This is why dream yoga does not begin at night. It depends on habits formed earlier.

If attention during the day is brittle, dependent on ideal conditions, it does not survive the transition into sleep. If attention is relaxed but steady, capable of reorienting itself amid change, it can appear spontaneously in dreams.

This appearance is not summoned. It is recognized.

Tibetan texts often describe dream awareness as arising naturally when conditions are present, rather than as something to be induced by force.[2] This framing matters because it protects the practice from striving.

The Role of Gentleness

Gentleness plays a critical role in attentional training for dream practice. A harsh relationship to attention creates tension. Tension disrupts sleep. Disrupted sleep fragments dreaming.

This is not a theoretical concern. Tibetan teachers repeatedly caution that excessive effort to achieve lucidity often leads to agitation, insomnia, or shallow sleep.[3] When this happens, the dream state becomes less accessible, not more.

Gentleness does not mean laxity. It means allowing attention to rest without gripping. This quality is cultivated during the day through practices that emphasize return rather than maintenance.

The practitioner learns to notice when attention has wandered and to come back without commentary. Over time, this pattern becomes familiar. It does not depend on verbal instruction. It becomes embodied.

At night, this familiarity allows awareness to surface briefly within the dream, without disrupting it.

Attention Without Fixation

Another important distinction concerns object-based attention. Many meditative practices train attention by fixing it on a single object. This can be useful for developing concentration, but dream yoga requires a different relationship to attention.

In dreams, objects are unstable. Forms shift quickly. Fixation collapses easily. If attention depends on holding a particular object in view, it is unlikely to persist.

Tibetan dream yoga, therefore, emphasizes awareness that is responsive rather than fixed. Attention remains present without becoming too tightly anchored to any single appearance. This allows recognition to occur even as the dream changes.

This approach aligns with broader Vajrayāna understandings of meditation, where awareness is trained to remain open and responsive rather than narrowly focused.[4] Dream practice extends this principle into sleep.

Distraction as Training

Distraction is not treated as failure. It is treated as material.

Every lapse of attention during the day becomes an opportunity to practice return. Each return strengthens the capacity to reorient without struggle. Over time, the mind becomes less reactive to its own movement.

This relationship to distraction carries into dreams. When attention is lost in a dream, it is lost completely. The dream proceeds without awareness. When attention returns, even momentarily, recognition can occur.

The emphasis is not on preventing loss, but on shortening the distance between loss and return.

This orientation protects the practitioner from discouragement. Dream awareness is intermittent by nature. Treating it as something that must be continuous leads to frustration. Tibetan sources consistently frame dream recognition as gradual and unpredictable.[5]

The Threshold of Recognition

Recognition in dreams often arises at moments of transition. A sudden shift in scenery. An impossible event. A break in narrative continuity. Attention, already trained to notice change without tightening, registers the incongruity.

When this happens, the dream does not necessarily become vivid or controllable. Often it remains ordinary. What changes is the relationship to it. The practitioner knows they are dreaming, but the dream continues.

This is sufficient.

The purpose of attention at this stage is not to sustain lucidity indefinitely. It is to make recognition possible at all. The training of attention prepares the ground. The dream supplies the conditions.

Preparing for Direct Practice

At this point in the book's progression, the necessary foundations are in place.

Illusion has been clarified as a condition to be worked with.

The continuity of mind across states has been established.

Dreams have been framed as a yogic field.

Ethical grounds and motivation have been addressed.

Attention has been trained to remain available without force.

Only now does it make sense to speak directly about lucidity.

The next chapter turns toward the first explicit encounters with dream awareness. These encounters are described phenomenologically rather than instructionally. The aim is to understand what recognition feels like before deliberately cultivating it.

Dream yoga proceeds by understanding experience as it unfolds, not by imposing structure upon it.

CHAPTER 6: THE FIRST MOMENT OF RECOGNITION

Recognition in a dream does not arrive with certainty.

It arrives as a hesitation.

Something in the dream falters. A detail does not fit. An event unfolds without resistance. The mind pauses, not long enough to analyze, but long enough to notice that what is happening does not carry the same weight it once did.

This pause is brief. Often, it is barely remembered. Yet Tibetan dream yoga treats it as decisive.

What matters is not how long recognition lasts, but that it occurs at all.

Recognition Is Not Control

A common misunderstanding is that dream recognition announces itself in a dramatic way. Popular accounts describe sudden clarity, vivid imagery, or the exhilarating sense of command over the dream environment. Tibetan sources describe something quieter.

Recognition does not interrupt the dream.

It loosens the bond between experience and belief.

The dream continues. Characters speak. Emotion arises. Narrative coherence remains intact. What changes is the way the experience is held. The practitioner knows, without reflection, that what appears is a dream.

This knowing does not require thought. It is immediate, embodied, and fragile. It can dissolve at any moment.

Tibetan texts emphasize this fragility repeatedly.[1] Recognition is not a state to be entered and maintained. It is an event that occurs when conditions align. Treating it as an achievement only ensures its disappearance.

Awareness *In* the Dream

It is important to distinguish awareness *of* the dream from awareness *in* the dream.

Awareness of the dream occurs after waking. It is reflective. The dream is recalled, interpreted, or evaluated. This kind of awareness is common and can be insightful, but it is not dream yoga.

Awareness in the dream occurs as the experience unfolds. It does not stand outside the dream. It is embedded within it. The practitioner does not observe the dream as an object. They recognize its nature from within.

This distinction is central to Tibetan treatments of dream yoga and is one of the points where misunderstanding is most common.[2] Recognition is not meta-cognition imposed from above. It is a shift in how appearance is apprehended.

The dream does not become transparent when analyzed. It becomes transparent because belief relaxes.

. . .

How Recognition Arises

Recognition tends to arise at moments of transition. A sudden change of scene. An impossible movement. A break in narrative logic. These moments disrupt habitual expectation, allowing attention to register what is normally overlooked.

Importantly, recognition does not arise from the practitioneris search for it. Searching tightens attention and reinforces control. Recognition arises because attention has been trained to remain available without fixation.

This is why the previous chapters matter.

Ethical ground reduces internal conflict.

Attentional stability allows awareness to remain present amid change.

Dreams, already fluid, supply the instability recognition requires.

When these conditions converge, recognition can occur spontaneously.

Tibetan sources consistently caution that deliberate attempts to "become lucid" often delay this process.[3] The more the practitioner tries to force recognition, the more the dream resists.

The Felt Quality of Recognition

The first moment of recognition is often understated. It may be accompanied by mild surprise, a sense of lightness, or a subtle release of tension. Rarely does it produce excitement. When excitement appears, recognition usually collapses soon after.

This is not a failure. It is part of the learning process.

Recognition introduces a new relationship to experience, but that relationship is unstable at first. Habitual responses reassert themselves quickly. The dream resumes its authority. Awareness fades.

Tibetan dream yoga does not treat this as a loss. It treats it as contact.

Each moment of recognition leaves an imprint. The mind learns, not conceptually but experientially, that appearance and belief are not identical. Over time, this learning accumulates.

Recognition Without Manipulation

At this stage, Tibetan sources advise restraint. Once recognition occurs, the temptation to manipulate the dream is strong. Forms can be altered. Fear can be escaped. Desire can be indulged.

This temptation is precisely why manipulation is postponed.

Manipulating the dream reinforces the sense of authorship. It shifts attention away from recognition and toward control. Tibetan traditions emphasize that the value of recognition lies in remaining present without interference.[4]

The dream is allowed to unfold. The practitioner stays with whatever arises. Fear is not avoided. Desire is not gratified. The aim is not to improve the dream, but to understand how experience persuades.

This restraint differentiates dream yoga from many modern approaches to lucid dreaming. The goal is not freedom within the dream, but insight into the nature of experience itself.

When Recognition Fails

Most dreams pass without recognition. This is expected. Tibetan sources repeatedly emphasize patience and proportion. Dream recognition is intermittent even for seasoned practitioners.

Failure, in this context, is not the absence of lucidity. It is the absence of reflection about conditions.

After waking, the practitioner considers not the content of the dream, but the quality of attention preceding sleep. Was the mind scattered? Was the motivation clear? Was restraint present during the day?

This reflection is not evaluative. It is diagnostic.

Dream yoga proceeds by understanding conditions, not by accumulating successes.

Recognition and the Path

The first moment of recognition does not transform the practitioner. It does not dissolve illusion permanently. What it does is establish a possibility.

Once the mind has recognized appearance as appearance within the dream, it knows that this recognition is possible. That knowledge does not disappear. It alters the horizon of practice.

This is why Tibetan sources treat early recognition with such care. It is not to be exaggerated or dismissed. It is to be protected.

The next chapter turns toward what follows recognition. How awareness remains present without collapsing into control. How the dream becomes a place of training rather than escape.

Recognition opens the path.

It does not complete it.

CHAPTER 7: REMAINING WITHIN THE DREAM

This chapter concerns what follows recognition.

Not how recognition is produced, and not how it is prolonged, but how it is *held* once it appears.

When a dream is recognized as a dream, the most difficult work begins.

The impulse to act is immediate. Once the dream is known as appearance, its apparent limits loosen. Fear could be escaped. Desire could be fulfilled. The dream world appears open to revision.

Tibetan dream yoga treats this moment with particular care.

Recognition does not authorize action.

It suspends it.

What is trained here is not freedom within the dream, but fidelity to recognition itself.

Non-Interference as Discipline

After recognition arises, Tibetan sources consistently advise restraint. The practitioner is instructed to allow the dream to continue without attempting to alter, escape, or improve it.[1]

This instruction is often misunderstood as passivity. It is nothing of the sort.

Non-interference is an active discipline. It is the deliberate refusal to reassert authorship over experience. When the dream is manipulated, agency returns quietly but decisively. The practitioner becomes the one who acts, directs, and chooses. Recognition gives way to control, and control reinstates belief.[2]

Remaining within the dream without interference preserves the conditions for recognition to deepen. The dream is not corrected. It is allowed to show itself.

Transformation Without Control

At this stage, a distinction becomes essential.

Control seeks to change what appears.

Transformation changes how what appears is held.

Tibetan dream yoga is oriented entirely toward the second.

A frightening image may remain frightening. A compelling scene may continue to unfold. What changes is not the dream's content, but the grip it exerts. Fear is felt without panic. Desire arises without compulsion. The dream continues, but its authority weakens.

This difference can be understood as a movement away from authorship. The practitioner does not stand outside the dream as its architect. They remain within it as participants, present without directing. Recognition deepens not by doing more, but by interfering less.

Fear Without Escape

Fear occupies a central place in dream practice. It arises quickly and convincingly, often without warning. In waking life, fear is frequently managed through avoidance or distraction. Dreams offer fewer exits.

Tibetan sources treat this not as a problem, but as an opportunity.[3] When fear is met without flight or suppression, its constructed nature becomes visible. The body reacts. Emotion surges. Yet belief loosens.

Fear persuades through urgency rather than truth.

By remaining present without escaping, the practitioner learns something difficult to learn during the day: that fear can be experienced without being obeyed. This learning does not remain confined to the dream. It reshapes how fear is encountered in waking life, where its operations are often subtler but no less compelling.

Desire and the Quiet Return of Identity

Desire presents a more subtle challenge.

When recognition arises, the dream often feels newly open. Possibility expands. The temptation to act increases. Tibetan traditions caution strongly at this point. Acting on desire within the dream quickly reconstitutes identity. The practitioner becomes the one who knows and uses the dream.[4]

This return of authorship is rarely noticed. It feels like freedom.

Remaining within desire without acting upon it requires restraint rather than repression. The aim is not moral purity. It is epistemic honesty. Desire reveals how swiftly identity reforms around preference and control.

When desire is allowed to arise without indulgence, its persuasive force weakens. The dream continues, but its pull diminishes.

The Fragility of Recognition

Recognition rarely persists for long. Excitement, fear, or subtle pride often disrupt it. Awareness collapses back into narrative. The dream regains its authority.

Tibetan dream yoga treats this collapse as expected. Loss of recognition is not failure. What matters is how it is met.

If recognition dissolves into frustration, fixation strengthens.

If it dissolves without agitation, its imprint remains.

For this reason, Tibetan sources emphasize gentleness after waking. Reflection is quiet and diagnostic rather than evaluative. Conditions are noted. Expectations are released.

Remaining within the dream includes remaining with its loss.

From Event to Posture

With time, recognition begins to shift. It no longer appears only as a dramatic event. Awareness becomes more evenly distributed across experience. The practitioner does not wait for lucidity. Presence moves with the dream as it unfolds.

The dream does not need to be held.

It is met.

This maturation aligns with broader Vajrayāna understandings of meditation as participation rather than observation. Awareness does not stand apart from experience. It remains intimate with it.

At this stage, the dream becomes less compelling, not because it disappears, but because it persuades less. Appearances arise and dissolve with less friction.

This shift cannot be forced. It emerges through repeated contact with recognition and restraint.

Preparing for Transformation

Remaining within the dream is not the end of practice. It is the condition that makes deeper work possible.

Once recognition stabilizes without collapsing into control, appearance itself becomes workable. Transformation no longer threatens to become manipulation. Compassion can arise without authorship. Insight can deepen without interference.

The next chapter turns directly to this transformation. It examines how appearances may change without reasserting control, and how the dream becomes a place of genuine practice rather than escape.

CHAPTER 8: TRANSFORMATION WITHOUT MANIPULATION

Once recognition stabilizes without collapsing into control, appearance itself becomes workable.

This does not mean that the dream becomes a canvas for invention. Tibetan dream yoga is explicit on this point. Transformation is not pursued in order to improve the experience or make it more agreeable. It arises from insight, not as a goal in itself.

The danger at this stage is subtle. Recognition has already loosened belief. Non-interference has prevented the reassertion of authorship. What now appears is the possibility that change might occur without effort.

This possibility must be approached carefully.

When Appearances Begin to Shift

In Tibetan sources, the transformation of dream appearances is described as occurring naturally once fixation weakens. Forms may soften. Threatening images may lose coherence. Boundaries between self and environment may become less distinct.[1]

These changes are not intentional. They are byproducts of recognition.

When belief no longer holds appearances rigidly in place, they become less constrained. The dream responds not to command, but to the absence of grasping. In this sense, transformation reflects the logic of emptiness already discussed earlier in the book. Appearances change because they were never fixed to begin with.

Importantly, Tibetan traditions emphasize that not all dreams transform in this way. Some remain vivid and compelling. Others dissolve quickly. The value of transformation is not measured by frequency or intensity, but by what it reveals about the nature of experience.

The Difference Between Allowing and Making

A crucial distinction emerges here.

Allowing refers to the relaxation of fixation.

Making refers to the reintroduction of agency.

The transformation that arises through allowing does not strengthen identity. Transformation produced through making. The former deepens recognition. The latter undermines it.

This distinction explains why Tibetan dream yoga delays any discussion of intentional transformation until recognition and non-interference are stable. Without that stability, attempts to change the dream merely rehearse the habit of control.

Tibetan commentarial sources repeatedly caution that deliberate manipulation at this stage often results in subtle contraction rather than freedom.[2] The dream may appear more pliable, but the practitioner becomes more invested.

Compassion Without Authorship

One of the most significant implications of transformation without manipulation concerns compassion.

In some Tibetan traditions, dream practice eventually includes compassionate engagement with dream figures. This engagement is often misunderstood as an intervention or a rescue. In fact, it is framed as presence without appropriation.

When recognition is stable, appearances are no longer taken as separate or self-existing. Compassion arises not as an act performed by a subject, but as a response that does not reinforce division. The practitioner does not fix the dream. They meet it.

This distinction matters because compassion enacted through authorship reintroduces hierarchy. Compassion arising without authorship dissolves it.

Tibetan sources emphasize that such engagement cannot be willed. It emerges when fixation has loosened sufficiently for responsiveness to occur without the need for strategy.[3]

When Transformation Does Not Occur

It is important to say plainly that transformation does not always follow recognition. Many dreams remain unchanged even when awareness is present. Tibetan traditions do not treat this as a problem.

The absence of transformation can itself be instructive. It reveals where belief remains strong. It shows where grasping still operates. Attempting to force change in such cases only obscures this information.

Dream yoga proceeds by listening to conditions rather than overriding them.

This orientation differentiates Tibetan approaches from systems that equate progress with increasingly dramatic dream control. In Tibetan dream yoga, dramatic change is not evidence of depth. Clarity of the relationship is.

Transformation and the Daytime World

The most important transformations occur outside the dream.

As recognition and non-interference mature, waking experience begins to shift in parallel ways. Situations feel less solid. Emotional reactions loosen more quickly. The urge to correct or control experience weakens.

These changes are often subtle. They do not announce themselves as insight. They appear as increased patience, responsiveness, and flexibility. Tibetan sources emphasize that this carryover is the real measure of dream practice.[4]

Transformation within the dream matters only insofar as it reshapes how experience is met elsewhere.

The Risk of Fascination

At this stage, fascination becomes a genuine risk. The mind may become preoccupied with unusual dream experiences or with the possibility of further transformation. Tibetan traditions consistently warn against this tendency.

Fascination pulls attention away from recognition and toward accumulation. The dream becomes something to acquire rather than a place of training. This shift is easy to miss because it often feels inspiring rather than grasping.

The discipline established in earlier chapters remains essential here. Transformation without manipulation depends on restraint, even when experience becomes more fluid.

Toward Integration

Transformation marks neither the end nor the goal of dream yoga. It signals a change in how appearances function when belief loosens, and control recedes.

The next chapter turns toward limits and risks. Tibetan traditions do not present dream yoga as universally beneficial or appropriate. Misunderstanding at this stage can undo earlier stability.

Before turning fully toward integration, it is necessary to address where dream practice can go wrong, and why restraint remains central even when insight deepens.

CHAPTER 9: LIMITS, RISKS, AND MISUNDERSTANDINGS

Dream yoga is often described in terms of possibility. What it makes visible. What it loosens. What does it allow to change? Tibetan traditions are careful to balance this emphasis with restraint. Not because the practice is fragile, but because it is easily misunderstood.

The risks of dream practice do not lie primarily in dreams themselves. They lie in how meaning is assigned to experience, and in how identity quietly reorganizes around unusual states.

For this reason, Tibetan sources consistently frame dream yoga as conditional. It is appropriate only under certain circumstances, for certain temperaments, and for certain motivations. Outside these conditions, it tends to magnify confusion rather than dissolve it.

Mistaking Experience for Insight

One of the most common misunderstandings is equating unusual experience with realization.

Vivid dreams, lucid episodes, and dramatic transformations of appearance can be compelling. They can also be misleading. Tibetan traditions are explicit that experience, no matter how striking, is not itself evidence of insight.[1]

Insight concerns the relationship, not the content.

When experience becomes the measure of progress, attention turns outward. The practitioner begins to evaluate dreams according to intensity, novelty, or control. This evaluation subtly reintroduces authorship and comparison. The dream becomes a source of identity rather than a field of recognition.

This shift often occurs quietly. It may even be encouraged by well-meaning fascination. Tibetan sources treat it as a sign that the practice has drifted from its purpose.

Inflation and Subtle Identity

Dream practice carries a particular risk of inflation. Because dreams are private and vivid, they can easily become proof of specialness. The practitioner may begin to see themselves as advanced, gifted, or uniquely capable.

This inflation does not require overt pride. It can appear as quiet certainty or subtle entitlement. Tibetan teachers consistently warn that such shifts are difficult to detect precisely because they feel like confidence.

Inflation undermines recognition by solidifying the sense that a practitioner knows, has experience, and possesses insight. Once this structure forms, dream practice reinforces it rather than loosens it.

For this reason, Tibetan traditions repeatedly emphasize humility and concealment. Dream experiences are not broadcast or displayed. They are integrated quietly, or not at all.

Psychological Vulnerability

Another risk concerns psychological stability.

Dream practice intensifies contact with unconscious material. Emotional themes that are muted during the day may surface vividly at night. For individuals with unresolved trauma, unstable mood, or fragile identity structures, this intensification can be destabilizing.

Tibetan traditions do not frame this as a moral failing. It is a matter of capacity. Dream yoga is not recommended universally, and it is often delayed or withheld when emotional stability has not been established.[2]

This caution distinguishes Tibetan dream yoga from contemporary approaches that present lucid dreaming as harmless or universally beneficial. Tibetan sources are explicit that some minds benefit from restraint rather than exposure.

Attachment to Control

As discussed in earlier chapters, control is the most persistent temptation in dream practice. Even when recognition is present, the urge to manipulate appearance can return subtly and repeatedly.

This attachment to control may present itself as experimentation or curiosity. Tibetan traditions do not condemn curiosity, but they insist on clarity about its effects. When control becomes central, recognition recedes.

The dream then becomes a space where agency is rehearsed rather than questioned. Over time, this rehearsal reinforces exactly what the practice is meant to dissolve.

Overextending the Meaning of Dreams

Another common misreading involves interpretation.

Because dreams feel meaningful, there is a temptation to treat them as messages to be decoded. Tibetan dream yoga does not prioritize symbolic interpretation. While Tibetan traditions include rich symbolic systems, dream yoga is not primarily interpretive.

Treating dreams as messages shifts attention away from how experience is constructed and toward what it supposedly signifies. This shift reintroduces belief at a different level.

Tibetan sources consistently redirect attention from meaning to process. What matters is not what the dream says, but how it persuades.[3]

When to Step Back

Perhaps the most important discipline in dream yoga is knowing when not to practice.

Tibetan traditions recognize periods when dream practice should be suspended. Excessive agitation, insomnia, emotional volatility, or fixation on experience are all signs that restraint is needed.

Stepping back is not regression. It is responsiveness.

The aim of dream yoga is not continuity of practice, but continuity of clarity. When practice undermines clarity, it ceases to serve its purpose.

Reaffirming the Orientation

The cautions described here are not meant to discourage. They are meant to preserve the integrity of the path.

Dream yoga is subtle work. It operates at the intersection of identity, imagination, and desire. Without restraint, it becomes entangled with the very structures it seeks to reveal.

With restraint, it becomes one of the most precise ways of learning how experience forms and persuades.

The final chapters turn toward integration. Dream practice does not end in dreams. Its value is measured by how it reshapes waking life, ethical responsiveness, and the capacity to meet experience without grasping.

Before that integration can be understood, the limits of the practice must be clearly seen.

CHAPTER 10: INTEGRATION: WHEN THE NIGHT INFORMS THE DAY

Dream yoga does not culminate in dreams.

Its value is measured by what changes elsewhere. By how experience is met when recognition is absent. By how belief loosens not only in the night, but in the ordinary pressures of the day.

For this reason, Tibetan traditions consistently frame dream practice as preparatory rather than complete. Dreams provide a condensed environment where the mechanisms of experience become visible. They reveal how quickly belief forms, how easily identity returns, and how fragile recognition can be. But the work does not remain confined there.

Integration begins when these lessons move beyond the dream.

Recognition Without the Frame of the Dream

In dreams, recognition is supported by instability. Scenes shift abruptly. Logic fractures. The unreliability of appearance is easier to glimpse.

Waking life offers fewer such openings. Appearances are more consistent. Narratives hold. Identity is reinforced by repetition and social agreement. For this reason, recognition rarely arises in the same way during the day.

Integration does not require it to do so.

What carries over is not lucidity, but sensitivity. The practitioner begins to notice how belief forms around perception. How reactions arise before they are named. How urgency persuades more than truth.

Moments that once passed unnoticed begin to register. A surge of irritation. A familiar fear. The impulse to correct, defend, or withdraw. These are not treated as problems to be solved. They are treated as appearances to be met.

The training of dream yoga lies precisely here. Not in reproducing nocturnal recognition during the day, but in recognizing the same dynamics at work.

The Softening of Authority

One of the most reliable signs of integration is a shift in authority.

Experience begins to persuade less. Thoughts lose some of their weight. Emotional reactions still arise, but they do not command in the same way. The practitioner finds themselves less compelled to resolve the experience immediately.

This does not produce indifference. It produces space.

Within that space, response becomes possible without rehearsal. Action occurs without the same level of investment in the outcome. Mistakes are made without the same need for justification.

This softening is often subtle. It does not announce itself as insight. It may appear as patience or as a slight delay before reaction. It may be noticed only in retrospect.

Tibetan traditions emphasize that such changes matter more than any dream experience. They indicate that recognition is no longer confined to a particular state. It has begun to inform posture.

Ethics Without Performance

Integration also reshapes ethical life.

When recognition remains confined to dreams, ethics can remain conceptual. Values are affirmed. Intentions are stated. But behavior changes little.

As dream practice matures, ethics becomes less about adherence and more about responsiveness. The practitioner becomes more sensitive to the effects of action. Not because rules are remembered, but because reactivity is seen sooner.

This does not lead to moral perfection. It leads to fewer justifications.

Harm is noticed earlier. Defensiveness weakens more quickly. Repair becomes possible without humiliation. Tibetan traditions treat this ethical responsiveness as a sign that insight has moved beyond experience and into relationship.

Without this movement, dream practice risks becoming insulated. With it, the practice begins to breathe.

When Practice Becomes Ordinary

A common misunderstanding is that integration makes practice more dramatic.

The Night as Path

In fact, it often makes it quieter.

The practitioner may find themselves less interested in extraordinary states. Dreams may become less vivid or less memorable. Recognition may occur less frequently at night.

This is not a loss.

As integration deepens, the distinction between practice and life becomes less sharp. Attention is no longer organized around producing recognition. It becomes available to what is present.

Dreams continue to teach, but they are no longer privileged. Waking experience becomes equally instructive. Both are treated as fields where belief arises and dissolves.

At this stage, dream yoga no longer stands apart. It becomes one expression of a broader orientation toward experience.

The End of Seeking in Dreams

One of the final shifts integration brings is the loosening of seeking.

The practitioner no longer looks to dreams for confirmation, advancement, or reassurance. Recognition is no longer treated as something to be collected or repeated.

Dreams are allowed to be ordinary.

This ordinariness is not a diminishment. It reflects a shift in motivation. Practice is no longer driven by the hope of special experience. It is sustained by interest in how experience functions.

Tibetan traditions regard this shift as a form of maturation. When dreams no longer need to impress, they can inform.

Returning to the Beginning

Dream yoga begins with recognition. It ends with familiarity.

Familiarity with how belief forms. Familiarity with how control returns. Familiarity with how experience persuades. This familiarity does not eliminate illusion. It changes the relationship to it.

The night teaches what the day conceals. The day tests what the night reveals.

Between them, a path takes shape. Not dramatic. Not linear. But precise.

Dream yoga offers no escape from experience. It offers a way of meeting it without grasping.

That meeting does not end when the dream dissolves. It continues wherever experience arises.

The work, finally, is not to remain lucid in dreams. It is to live without being fully persuaded.

CONCLUSION: THE NIGHT AS PATH

Dream yoga is often approached as a method for altering experience. This book has argued for something quieter and more demanding.

Dreams matter not because they are extraordinary, but because they reveal how experience persuades. They show how belief forms, how identity reasserts itself, and how quickly recognition can be replaced by control. They compress these processes into a setting where their mechanics are easier to see.

What is learned there does not belong to the night.

Throughout these chapters, recognition has been treated not as a state to be maintained, but as an event that interrupts habit. It appears briefly, often without fanfare, and disappears just as easily. Its significance lies not in duration or intensity, but in what it makes possible. Once recognition has occurred, even fleetingly, experience is no longer entirely convincing in the same way.

This shift is subtle. It does not dismantle illusion. It loosens allegiance to it.

For this reason, restraint has remained central throughout the discussion. Without restraint, recognition collapses into authorship. Control replaces intimacy. Experience becomes something to be improved rather than understood. Dream yoga then reinforces the very structures it aims to expose.

With restraint, something else becomes possible. Experience is allowed to show itself without correction. Fear arises without urgency. Desire appears without command. Identity reforms and dissolves in plain view. Over time, familiarity replaces fascination.

This familiarity is the real fruit of the practice.

It is not a special capacity. It does not guarantee insight or stability. It does not confer authority. What it offers is orientation. The practitioner becomes less interested in what experience contains and more interested in how it functions. Appearance is no longer taken at face value, but neither is it dismissed.

Dream yoga, understood in this way, does not stand apart from the broader contemplative path. It sharpens it. By revealing the mechanics of belief in a condensed environment, it prepares the ground for a different relationship to waking life.

That relationship is not defined by detachment. It is defined by responsiveness.

As recognition matures, the boundary between dream and day becomes less decisive. Not because the two are equated, but because the same dynamics are recognized in both. Urgency persuades. Control reassures. Identity reforms quietly. And belief relaxes when it is no longer obeyed automatically.

The night teaches what the day conceals. The day tests what the night reveals.

In this sense, the night is not an escape from life. It is a path through it. A path that does not bypass illusion, but learns how it operates. A path that does not promise certainty, but cultivates clarity about how certainty is manufactured.

Dream yoga does not aim to make life lighter. It aims to make it less rigid. Less compelled. Less governed by the need to secure experience.

The work it invites is ongoing. Recognition must be met again and again. Restraint must be renewed. Familiarity deepens slowly, often unnoticed.

What changes is not the world of appearance, but the weight it carries.

That is the path the night offers.

A NOTE TO THE READER

If this book has been meaningful to you, a brief review can help it reach readers who are looking for this kind of work.

Reviews do not need to be long or evaluative. A few sentences describing how the book met you, or what it clarified for you, are enough. You can leave a review wherever you purchased or discovered the book.

Thank you for taking the time to read with care.

NOTES

Chapter 2: The Subtle Mind and the Continuity of Awareness

1. Herbert V. Guenther, *The Dawn of Tantra* (Berkeley: Shambhala, 1975), 63–67.
2. B. Alan Wallace, *Dreaming Yourself Awake: Lucid Dreaming and Tibetan Dream Yoga* (Boston: Wisdom Publications, 1999), 21–29.
3. B. Alan Wallace, *Dreaming Yourself Awake: Lucid Dreaming and Tibetan Dream Yoga* (Boston: Wisdom Publications, 1999), 21–29.
4. Tenzin Wangyal Rinpoche, *The Tibetan Yogas of Dream and Sleep* (Ithaca, NY: Snow Lion Publications, 1998), 45–52.

Chapter 3: Dreams as a Yogic Field

1. Georges B. J. Dreyfus, *Recognizing Reality: Dharmakīrti's Philosophy and Its Tibetan Interpretations* (Albany: State University of New York Press, 1997), 301–305.
2. B. Alan Wallace, *Dreaming Yourself Awake: Lucid Dreaming and Tibetan Dream Yoga* (Boston: Wisdom Publications, 1999), 83–87.
3. Tenzin Wangyal Rinpoche, *The Tibetan Yogas of Dream and Sleep* (Ithaca, NY: Snow Lion Publications, 1998), 89–94.
4. Andrew Holecek, *Dream Yoga: Illuminating Your Life Through Lucid Dreaming and the Tibetan Yogas of Sleep* (Boulder, CO: Sounds True, 2016), 141–147.

Chapter 4: Ethical Ground and Motivation

1. Tsongkhapa, *The Great Treatise on the Stages of the Path to Enlightenment (Lamrim Chenmo)*, vol. 1, trans. Joshua W. C. Cutler et al. (Ithaca, NY: Snow Lion Publications, 2000), 209–215.
2. B. Alan Wallace, *Dreaming Yourself Awake: Lucid Dreaming and Tibetan Dream Yoga* (Boston: Wisdom Publications, 1999), 118–122.
3. Patrul Rinpoche, *The Words of My Perfect Teacher*, trans. Padmakara Translation Group (Boston: Shambhala, 1994), 145–149.
4. Tenzin Wangyal Rinpoche, *The Tibetan Yogas of Dream and Sleep* (Ithaca, NY: Snow Lion Publications, 1998), 101–106.
5. Georges B. J. Dreyfus, "The Sound of Two Hands Clapping: The Education of a Tibetan Buddhist Monk," *Journal of the American Academy of Religion* 65, no. 3 (1997): 515–517.

Notes

Chapter 5: Attention and Stability

1. Tsongkhapa, *The Great Treatise on the Stages of the Path to Enlightenment (Lamrim Chenmo)*, vol. 3, trans. Joshua W. C. Cutler et al. (Ithaca, NY: Snow Lion Publications, 2004), 25–31.
2. B. Alan Wallace, *Dreaming Yourself Awake: Lucid Dreaming and Tibetan Dream Yoga* (Boston: Wisdom Publications, 1999), 132–136.
3. Tenzin Wangyal Rinpoche, *The Tibetan Yogas of Dream and Sleep* (Ithaca, NY: Snow Lion Publications, 1998), 112–118.
4. Herbert V. Guenther, *The Tantric View of Life* (Boulder, CO: Shambhala, 1972), 87–90.
5. Andrew Holecek, *Dream Yoga: Illuminating Your Life Through Lucid Dreaming and the Tibetan Yogas of Sleep* (Boulder, CO: Sounds True, 2016), 167–172.

Chapter 6: The First Moment of Recognition

1. Tenzin Wangyal Rinpoche, *The Tibetan Yogas of Dream and Sleep* (Ithaca, NY: Snow Lion Publications, 1998), 129–134.
2. B. Alan Wallace, *Dreaming Yourself Awake: Lucid Dreaming and Tibetan Dream Yoga* (Boston: Wisdom Publications, 1999), 145–151.
3. Andrew Holecek, *Dream Yoga: Illuminating Your Life Through Lucid Dreaming and the Tibetan Yogas of Sleep* (Boulder, CO: Sounds True, 2016), 193–198.
4. Tsongkhapa, *The Great Treatise on the Stages of the Path to Enlightenment (Lamrim Chenmo)*, vol. 3, trans. Joshua W. C. Cutler et al. (Ithaca, NY: Snow Lion Publications, 2004), 345–348.

Chapter 7: Remaining Within the Dream

1. Tenzin Wangyal Rinpoche, *The Tibetan Yogas of Dream and Sleep* (Ithaca, NY: Snow Lion Publications, 1998), 143–149.
2. Śāntideva, *The Bodhicaryāvatāra*, trans. Kate Crosby and Andrew Skilton (Oxford: Oxford University Press, 1996), VI.23–28.
3. Patrul Rinpoche, *The Words of My Perfect Teacher*, trans. Padmakara Translation Group (Boston: Shambhala, 1994), 274–277.
4. B. Alan Wallace, *Dreaming Yourself Awake: Lucid Dreaming and Tibetan Dream Yoga* (Boston: Wisdom Publications, 1999), 168–173.

Chapter 9: Limits, Risks, and Misunderstandings

1. B. Alan Wallace, *Dreaming Yourself Awake: Lucid Dreaming and Tibetan Dream Yoga* (Boston: Wisdom Publications, 1999), 182–186; Patrul

Notes

Rinpoche, *The Words of My Perfect Teacher*, trans. Padmakara Translation Group (Boston: Shambhala, 1994), 289–293.
2. Tenzin Wangyal Rinpoche, *The Tibetan Yogas of Dream and Sleep* (Ithaca, NY: Snow Lion Publications, 1998), 162–168.
3. Georges B. J. Dreyfus, *Recognizing Reality: Dharmakīrti's Philosophy and Its Tibetan Interpretations* (Albany: State University of New York Press, 1997), 324–328.

www.ingramcontent.com/pod-product-compliance
Lightning Source LLC
Chambersburg PA
CBHW060505080526
44584CB00015B/1553